PSALM TO WHOM(E)

PSALM TO WHOM(E)

DIANE GLANCY

TURTLE POINT PRESS

BROOKLYN, NEW YORK

Requests for permissions to make
copies of any part of the work should
be sent to:
Turtle Point Press, 208 Java Street,
Fifth Floor, Brooklyn, NY, 11222
info@turtlepointpress.com

Library of Congress Catalogue-in-
Publication Data

Names: Glancy, Diane, author.
Title: Psalm to whom(e) / Diane
Glancy.
Description: First edition. |
Brooklyn, New York : Turtle Point
Press,
   2023.
Identifiers: LCCN 2023026615 |
ISBN 9781885983343 (paperback)
Subjects: LCGFT: Poetry.
Classification: LCC PS3557.L294
P77 2023 | DDC 811/.54--dc23/
eng/20230609
LC record available at https://lccn.
loc.gov/2023026615

Book design by Zab Hobart

Printed in the United States of
America

First Edition

PSALM TO WHOM(E)

QUILTLINE

PSALMS

JOHN THE BAPTIST AND THE CRITICAL WORK OF WRITING WITH SCAFFOLDING LEFT IN PLACE

QUILTING

INTRODUCTION

Psalm to Whom(e) is a book of hybrid poetry that encroaches on other genres— a Pokemon consuming what it comes near. A guild of similar interest in story-telling with its different voices. A junto.

Psalm to Whom(e) is a story of faction. Yet unity is there. A quilt-work of experience. A variegated covering for a bed of content.

Writing sometimes is a way of translating English into English. It's a way of stretching or pulling language until it becomes a transparency through which other things can be seen— old thought patterns, for instance— the early struggle to reconcile what is within oneself and what is outside. The struggle to reconcile the *I* and the *It*. And to seek the *Whom* who is supposed to be over all. In which to build shelter. To find *home*. Is it not primal thinking that made Picasso divide nose from face and ear from side of head. Is it not a form of thinking that results in writing that sometimes lays trap lines to catch a visage of the Old World nearly transferred into the existing world.

I give range to language for the purpose of finding sightings to the kind of information that was in the old language. I try to purpose oralities.

I'm interested in the warping of language I know so that the *otherness* I also know can be seen behind the words.

In the disruption of text— the disagreement of syntax— something *other* seems to work its way into the piece. An allusion striking resistance to the representational. Calling something without calling it. A quilt made of many pieces taken from diverse fabrics. The garments from which the pieces came still defined. Remembered. Though the garments no longer have form, the form is intrinsic to the unit of the piece-work quilt. Writing takes an accretion of incongruous layers to reach the undercurrents of meanings in the structure of concept and oralities.

ALLUSION

How land and octopus are similar. Holding with arms— or are they legs— those tentacles with suction that is gravity. Over which the land is layered— covering rock and molten core. Over which the ocean. The snowfalls. Ice caps. Volcano. The beak of earth. The land and the land with its voices from those tongueless places.

Just drive highway 90 across south Texas. Uvalde. Kinney. Val Verde. Terrell. Brewster. Presidio. In the isolation of a pandemic. You feel the land flat as any octopus can flatten itself. Land as large as the octopus that covers the ship in Pierre de Montfort's 1801 pen and wash drawing.

Land overgrown with bushes that hide an old farmhouse. Or tendrils on the grape vines. Or tentacles of memory the land brings forth. The place now vacant on the vacant land. The ground bramble you cannot walk.

The land and octopus as adversary.

Octopus from the Latin derived from Ancient Greek *okto* eight, *pous* foot.

Land from Middle English *lond*, from Old English long meaning earth, territory, land, soil, ground, ridge in a ploughed field, from Proto-Germanic *landa*, from Proto-Indo-European *lend*.

A place from which you are lent and returned. As if a library where a librarian had a pencil with a date-stamp instead of eraser. And the long narrow drawers of the old card catalogue were roads you wanted to travel.

The octopus is any splay of dirt roads off highway 90. Any sudden culvert, wash or canyon.

In the 5th century, Anaxogoras thought the world was flat and many with him who must have been in Texas. Octopodo could be any of those isolated, eight-building towns you pass.

DRIVING IN KANSAS AND TEXAS

DRIVING IN KANSAS

Late in June, I drove Highway 56 from Santa Fe to Kansas City backward along the 750 miles of the old Santa Fe Trail— northeast across the edge of New Mexico— the Oklahoma panhandle— and then the long drive from the southwest corner of Kansas to northeast border on a single-lane highway. Some of the towns: Moscow. Ulysses [the road to it]. Montezuma. Dodge. Larned. Pawnee Rock [mid-point between Missouri and New Mexico on the old Santa Fe Trail]. Great Bend. Quivira Wildlife Refuge, a town for migrating fowl [named for the Indians Francisco Vasquez de Coronado found in central Kansas in 1541] [before it was Kansas]. McPherson. Emporia. Shawnee Mission [an outpost of Kansas City].

In travel, I find the variables that vary with the weather. Temperature. Time of day. The shape of the land. Wind— clear or blowing dust from the fields, and as wind usually blows from the west and southwest, I was pushed along instead of facing headwinds. My interior landscape is another variable. Also the relationship of my inner landscape with the variables of the outer landscape on the land I pass.

I find different parts of myself on the backroads. I have to travel alone. It is where these parts of myself wait. They are hermits living in caves that appear when I pass them, then disappear again.

Often I visit the past. Memory is travel. Travel is memory. Situations are there. Travel triggers memory, which is another group of variables in the already varied travel. Even memory can change events.

Boredom is the wind in a bare field. It is boredom that drives out these hermits. In places that take closer attention to the road, I pay attention to my driving. On the open road of Kansas, on the utter flatness and plainness of the land, I travel other places.

I pass a calf standing in a corner of a field. Somewhere in my interior landscape another calf is standing in another corner of another field. These variables mesh and make more variables of experience. Where is the herd? Why is the calf by itself? The solemn center of the self is there. Abandoned. I feel the desolation that is there in Kansas, which is there in me. There is an isolation of life that sends me to faith. To the raw scrubbing I need to reckon with myself.

When I passed the Kansas fields earlier in the spring, many of them were underwater. The land was a shallow lake, but a lake nonetheless. Now later in the summer, the fields had dried and had not been planted. The wind takes its fingernail and lifts the crust of soil. Thus, the dust— and chaff [some of it] from the harvesters in other fields not flooded.

In travel, I see what cannot be seen unless I was on the road. Removed from the cover of ordinary life to the cover of ordinary driving. On a mission— as a Christian, to think of the suffering of Christ. I have been in Sunday school and the Protestant church all my life. I like the setting of sanctuary. It is like driving in a car. It is a part of nature. A wildlife refuge. The land and sky. The messaged air. The parts of its meaning pushing further into awareness. In the Bible belt, God is part of the landscape. God and distance are one.

God is a moving God. Transient while always being there. Unchangeable yet changing with situations in my life that need tending. He is here and he is there. And he is there in a different way than he is here. Because my life changes and needs a different God in different places, which he accommodates. He always is the same God, yet he is different in the different ways I face.

I travel to see what comes into my mind. Driving is a time of communion. Holy God. I am grateful. Everlasting God in whom I am well pleased.

I am on the road. Clouds in the whole sky hover above Kansas. The day [June 27] is hazy. Blowing dust and harvesting. Though it seems early in the summer for the large harvesters in the fields. Ahead, there is a harvester on the highway driving from one field to another, a long line of traffic behind it as though a line of ducklings.

A force moves forward on a highway across the land. The wildflowers not yet mowed. Or another generation of wildflowers if the ditches were earlier mowed. There is the indirect driving of getting somewhere also. A crossing of images that travel over the variations in the road. Be prepared to stop— one-lane ahead for road repairs. It is 94° at 2:30 in the afternoon.

I see Christ of the wheat fields in Kansas because I find desperation in travel— just enough to recognize it and not sink into it. On this particular trip, the round oil cars beside Highway 56 are disciples wrapped in black robes.

I could have taken Interstate 25 north to Denver and then I-70 east across Kansas. Instead I took the diagonal, single-lane backroad across Kansas, shorter in miles, but slower with speed limits and stop lights in small towns, and a line of trucks I could not always get around.

Bless the sea of fields. The imagined boat. Bless the high tide of Kansas and storms that swale the land. I travel and let the frustration wash up over me. Christ of the ever present. Keep me knowing you. There is a herd waiting for me somewhere— even if it is in the world to come.

All those times of rejection in the school row. My father transferred again and again in his work in the stockyards of the Midwest. In the moving my family did. The upheaval. The feeling of being separated from others. Hosanna to Christ of the sour wind from hog barns and cattle lots. Have mercy on us for the suffering we cause your creatures.

At one point of road construction, stopped in traffic, I am weary of travel. I turn off the air-conditioner and roll down the window as I wait to move forward.

I hear the wind playing in the field. The stalks of wheat shimmer. The weeds at the side of the road wave triumphantly. I listen to the shimming. It sounds a little like the surf. It is easier to walk on water here.

I like the barns I pass. I see them as prophets. I see them across Kansas through which I travel.

As a child I climbed in my grandfather's barn in Kansas. I still have the small, wooden wheel to the pulley that lifted hay bales to the loft. In Sunday school, I learned the first barn was an ark. Before the ark, there were shepherds, herders, desert nomads— maybe corrals of ropes tied between trees. They did not float.

Barns came to America with the first immigrants. They built Jamestown Colonists barns. New England saltbox barns. Pennsylvania Dutch barns. Barns moved west with the settlers. Homestead barns. Prairie gambrel barns. Raised monitor barns. Bank barn [built into a hill]. Kansas limestone and post rock barns. Standing in the fields— Isaiah, Jeremiah, Ezekiel.

A barn is a prophet in a square cloak. A barn has a weathervane on the peak of its hood. A barn is a quilt. A shelter for plow horse. Cow. A dog in winter. Sow. A barn is storage for fodder. Sunlight passes between the boards and travels across the barn floor as the sun moves across the sky above it. Birds are there.

Old English *bern* [*bere* from barley + *ern* house]. Old Frisian *fiaern*. Old High German *evin*. Gothic *razn*. Old Norse *rann*.

A barn is steadfast as a prophet in the heat and drought of summer. The storm and cold of winter. A barn is a messenger. Old barn-wood is prophecy. A barn is a library. The boards of a barn are volumes of books in their rows.

When passing over rough road the psalms are a prophet— Joel, Amos, Habakkuk.

The barns are my hiding place. They preserve me from the trouble of storms, coyotes, other predators. They compass me with sound when wind moans between the boards, the owls hoot, and other birds make their chirps— Psalm 32:1.

DRIVING IN TEXAS

You can drive 800 miles and still be in Texas [900 actually]. From the northwest corner of Texas 40 miles northwest of Dalhart, to Brownsville / South Padre Island is 900 miles. [Farther actually because the road often is not a straight line.]

There is a baseness that fills the land with itself until there is a completeness in the nothingness. The gesture of wind. The shunning. The brightness that is a being of its own.

In travel, there is the thought that the road is central. The road and more particular, the car can be interchanged with house in Gaston Bachelard's book *The Poetics of Space*.

For me, the house has a garage. In the garage is a car. Behind the car is a driveway. Connected to the driveway is a street. Follow enough streets and there is a highway.

When I sleep in my car on the road at night, I am with those who came before me, who left their encampments in the trunk of memory.

Travel by car is horizontal. A road goes from departure to destination. It is not up and down from attic to cellar in Bachelard's vertical construct. A road is forward. A getting to from-a-place to another place. A getting to from.

The roads in north central Texas are noncommittal. The land nondescript. Plains. Prairie. Scrub brush. Barren land. Washes. Dry creeks. Old sea floors. Fossils. Rocks. Fish bones. Pictographs. Pelicans— [electricity poles for voltage].

Driving in Texas there is the glare of the sun on bare, flat land. To the southwest, there is the respite of the hill country with its wildflowers. The Guadalupe Mountain Range 8,749 feet at its peak. The higher altitude of clouds. But Texas mostly is flat. Arid. Wide. Plain as a brown horse. The land and the sky. The sky and the land.

Driving covers roads not on the map. Driving long distances for a long time invents roads that are needed for transportation to destinations. Especially the roads that call one to look at what one is inside. Often with devastating vision. Sorrows of the past joining journeys of faith that [seemingly] wander in the desert. The rising of what needs to rise to be dealt with is a job of travel. The desert is not separated from mystery. The solitariness of land. The singularity. The investigational imagining. Enduring the trial of travel. The journey onward to the hurtful restart of that which has passed. Human interior is a rocky terrain.

From Bachelard— "The hermit is alone before God. His hut [car] therefore is just the opposite of a monastery. And there radiates about this centralized solitude a universe of meditation and prayer, a universe outside the universe."

It is the poverty of spirit that is called up in driving. As destination increases, it is the accumulation of images from within that gives access to arrival.

A road is a concentrated being. Traveling alone "gives us access to absolute refuge."

The "dual vertical polarity of a house" becomes the dual horizontal polarity of the car. I am moving. I am in stasis. I am in one place as I drive. I cannot get up unless the car is stopped. I am in a place defined by the structure of the car around me. Neither is the land moving as I pass. There is a large part of travel that stays where it is.

"A house [car] constitutes a body of images—" Travel is an intermediary.

The road is traveled indirectly. Each journey has other journeys within it.

Like a swallow I chatter— Isaiah 38:14. O bent God, I knock on your door. I hear you grieving. You made the world as you made it. But it went its own way. Its sorrows bend you as gravity bends light waves. You made yourself vulnerable when you gave us a will of our own. You had to invent a solution to our fall. It was Christ on the cross in whom is reconciliation. O God you are my harrowing— as the world is yours.

The small cliff-swallows return to the Frio River in southwest Texas after the last frost. They muffle the air with their quiet trilling, circling back and forth in chaotic patterns.

O God— your word comes in a flight pattern of its own.   23

You give us little insight into your mystery [who and what and where you are]. We have your book of many writers, many places, many subjects— one of which is certainly division— a book divided not only into chapters and verses, but into variables of theme and structure. In your book prophets howl at the people who have divided themselves from you.

What I want to say often comes in a flight pattern of its own.

At one time, the tribal people carried their history in memory.

There were carriers of memory that called their stories back from the beginning. The memory keeper would talk sometimes for days, incorporating the beginning of their emergence from a log or from underground or from wherever in their earliest tribal history. As if to tell a story in the New Testament, you had to begin in Genesis and continue through the Bible to the New Testament. Or to tell me what you did yesterday, you would start from the day of your birth.

The stories were told without written text. The spoken word always was separate from the written word as there was no writing to record— though pictographs, petroglyphs, teepee drawings and wampum belts depicted events.

Even now, as the word is written, it is separate from the written letters. The sound lifts above the page. It is abstract— as a wounding and tearing from the base. It is primitive as first efforts to align thought with written word—

"The Ball of Fire" translated from the Cherokee, *Cherokee Narratives: A Linguistic Study* by Durbin Feeling, William Pulte and Gregory Pulte, University of Oklahoma Press, 2018—

when I was growing up somewhere the year of not yet electricity we had no wiring in our home house we liked was near apart their home for us to go there television they had and nightly just almost a few families they would come and gather television for them to come one time midnight when we returned at home dog fiercely was uttering it was barking just as something here close by as if he were seeing it the same he was doing it was chasing after it over there distance and then he would turn back here close by he would return and his barking it would continue not much we didn't pay much attention to it at first that when it did that but the next day night same he did it he would chase after it over there distance and then he would turn back and then again he would chase after it just as though if he wanted someone to follow him and

at first just a cow or just something something else stock it
may be roaming we all thought then it made him curious my
father who was and gun big barrel he went and got in the house
and my brother and I my dad also then we followed it dog and
dog whenever when he realized that we were following him he
kept going no now he didn't turn back I then three of us we
all followed him and somewhere round one-fourth of a mile in
distance he went something as if he were chasing it just as big
oak tree he went around and up toward he was barking in the
fall time it was and leaves had fallen completely it was trees and
midnight sun dweller also brightly it was shining but we went
completely around oak tree and not also something perched on
we didn't see and dog continued fiercely uttering barking and
when we gave up something for us to see my dad who was then
at tree up toward he aimed big barrel gun and he shot and just
then you could say around flaming a ball the size of it went up
sky toward and just a few feet distance it faded from then on he
quit dog fiercely uttering his barking

The story is a magical happening in a narrative relating an ungrounded
method of story-telling that bypasses reason and maintains the essence
of the old tribal world transposed in English. [As when I read Gertrude
Stein's "I will not be often betrayed by delayed / Not often / Nor when
they cherish which not often" and James Joyce's "I have sinned: or no: I
have suffered it is. And the other one: iron nails ran in."]

"The Ball of Fire" is a story of the light that left this world.

I visited a neighbor's house also for television.

But more I could identify with the word order. The association and
dissociation. The scrape of repetition and the splaying of thought. Like
cliff-swallows above the Frio River in southwest Texas at Laity Lodge off
Highway 83 during an annual retreat of Chrysostom, a writer's group I
have belonged to for years.

Overly God. I knock on your door but you are in council.

O God over all. According to your word there is no other God but you. As the tribes of Native people all say they are the first people. As all gods say they are the only god. You are force and you are grace. It is a going of both ways. As cars forward and backward across the land at the same time. A sense of terrain as an oppositional being. A military mind brought home to the people here. An exactness over which there is no leniency. As driving on a road alone in a car.

Middle English and Old Norman French *carre*. Late Latin *carrum*. Latin *carrus* [original two-wheeled Celtic war chariot]. Gaul *carros*. Old Irish *carr*. Indo-European *krsos*. Any vehicle on wheels.

In photographs of the trips to my grandparent's farm, the car is in them. My father and my uncles stood by their cars. Their wives and children also. There are few photographs of the family before the farmhouse flocked by tall hollyhocks and morning glory. It was the car that was the base of structure— from the backseat as a child, to the passenger seat as a wife, to the driver's seat as a person of my own.

As if all life were meant for departure.

On a sad day I parked the car when I went to lunch and saw morning glories on a fence. They had been on my grandparent's farm in Kansas. For a moment the childhood visits to the farm returned. I remembered wandering in solitude around the farm.

Now I drive in Texas where I also live.

In Texas the barns are metal Butler Buildings. They have no gutters. I hear the rain that falls off the building where I live in Texas on my son's place. A county road. A house. Sheds. Pasture. Horse. A barn that is a Butler Building renovated into living quarters with a garage for car, truck, tractor, welder.

Southwest Texas on the map is blank. Nothing there. As if a snowfall in the desert. As if whited-out on the map. Not even bull riders or cowboys. The hustle of wind and dust. A few cattle on open range. The counties of Jeff Davis, Presidio, Pecos, Brewster, Terrell, Vel Verde. All south of I-10 the bottom hem of Texas. All hanging on nothing. Yet there is the ghosts of old roads— the San Antonio – El Paso Road. The Pecos River – New Mexico Road. The Comanche Trail to Chihuahua, Mexico. The Butterfield Overland Mail Route.

Fort Stockton was established in 1859 as a stop-over at Comanche Springs. Confederates took possession of the fort in 1861. In 1867, the Army rebuilt Fort Stockton for an Indian Wars Fort that was garrisoned until 1886.

In the silence, I still can hear the soldiers, freight wagons, cattle drives, stockmen, laborers, merchants, Indians.

I drive back and forth from Kansas to Texas. It is hard not to travel where wranglers have led with ongoings backward and forward until the abrupt stop when I pull into the garage in Kansas or the barn in Texas.

I suppose you can drive 800 miles in Kansas too— if you start from the Missouri border and drive 400 miles west to the Colorado border and turn around and drive 400 miles back to the Missouri border.

SEVERANCE

Angle. It will be a life of struggle with no consummation.
3/14/47, *A Prayer Journal,*
FLANNERY O'CONNOR

TEXAS QUILT MUSEUM, LAGRANGE

These are the wounded.
The dismembered sleeves and trouser legs.
Veterans of ringer washers and clothesline hangings battered by wind.
These quilts nailed on the wall.
The pieces of fabric separated from what they had been.
Now stitched to other fabrics.
Vertical on the cross.
Transfigured in the afterlife.

SUMMONS

The tin roof of the shed.
The wind got into and rattled.
I heard in the distance.
Pine trees dropped their cones.
The sycamore and shagbark hickory their nuts.
The whirlwind spread the sky.
Elk circled.
The sun flattened on the edge of the hills.
The heavens are fiercer than imagined.
In an old story the sun gave birth to birds with wings that raked the fields.
Out across the pasture the sound of a tractor.
The coils of dust.
I took the bicycle pump to the sun.
Inflated again in the sky.

50 MILES WEST OF ABILENE TEXAS
NOVEMBER 7 2020

Because a deer on the interstate.
I hit in the dark.
And continued without looking.
To think it quickly in the next world.
The deer that made the dent.

When later it was light.
I found I could not open the door
but crawled to the other seat and opened the other door.
And saw the deer had dented the car and bent the headlight and front fender
and sent back along the first door and the second.

A deer-head in the headlight swift as a comet falling back along the car.
Gone before you think what to wish.

Coming from the canyon.
The pictographs in Seminole had gone there to see.
A shaman wearing the head of a deer.
Had traveled from the overhang of the cliff.

I go to those places of the other world.
To bring back my own.
Belonging to nothing otherwise.
The Savior a deer to me.
As it was in the headlight slain on the passing of the cross.
The door then opened to the other world.

TRIPOD

[1] FATHER ALFRED

It is said the earthquake is the migration of animals that cannot be seen. A stampede actually picking apart the foundation that falls.

He told them about the cross as they were quilting. Mostly it was dislocating as the work of assimilation.
Quilting is a brutal craft that begins with scissors. It is Christianity with its swords and thorns and nails. The names of quilts— *Sawtooth. Streak of Lightning. Shoo fly. Crucifixion. Crazy Quilt* with squares going everywhere. Without pattern. But the end is the preservation of cloth that otherwise would not be preserved.

In the earthquake buffalo hide is remembered. The bone needle and sinew. Now the paper bit me or maybe it is his needle in my hand. At night my grandmother talks to me about quilting.

There are rifts in the texts I read. Fissures underneath. These are the names of the quilts they made— *Fort Parker Massacre 1836. Battle of Plum Creek 1840. Battle of Palo Duro Canyon 1874. Battle of Yellow House Canyon 1877.*

[2] FATHER ALFRED

Maybe now it is him— wearing a horse mask with wooden ears— eyebrows held on with brass upholstery-studs and teeth that are stubs of dowel rods.

He lectures from the chalkboard on solecism— a word that refers to an ungrammatical combination usually of words— but also of thought.

Solecism is a dream-word. He is against it. We must learn to write clearly. We must give up our old language— though a thought walks two paths at once.

Does he not know a horse carried language to the earth because it was the heaviest load? Therefore a sentence starts with hooves.

He has four legs under his robe. In his sleep at night he neighs His room beneath theirs in the school. I am writing on my tablet. Near the end his legs kept running.

[3] THE STORYTELLER NAILS HER THESIS TO THE QUILTMAKER'S DOOR

In those days fabric was sparse. We held onto our clothes or she would cut them into pieces.

Near death her hand kept stitching. She sewed to the end of the road.

I stitch pieces together too— pieces of cloth that have been cut— that have been wounded in the cutting. Only my fabric is stories—

My mother had a taffeta skirt she kept it in the back of her closet. After she died, I found the skirt. When light shines on it, the skirt is like copper. When I wear the skirt I hear the deer-skin dresses with elk teeth sewn to them. I hear the jingle dresses with tobacco-can lids rolled into small cones— sewn close enough they speak when I move.

When did she wear the skirt? Where did she get it? How did she hide it from my grandmother, the quiltmaker?

Maybe my mother wore the skirt in a dream— floating above the bed until she found the window— flying out into the cold winter air.

I see her in the taffeta skirt. A large bird's head on her shoulders. Bird-claws sticking out beneath the skirt. My grandmother trying to capture her with thread and needle from a peddler who came to the reservation and continued up the dirt road.

Maybe my mother passes above me in the night. The taffeta smooth as tanned deer hide scraped with a worked stone.

I have two stones from a buffalo jump— one, an ordinary stone— the other with an indent for a thumb, a worked stone that scraped hide until it was transformed by the visceral work of cutting— of making something of the parts.

There may have been 100 million Indians on this continent when the Europeans landed. Ninety percent were killed by smallpox, cholera, tuberculosis, measles, massacre.

I hear my grandmother's spirit-voice from the next world— she does not approve. I tell her we work in our different ways— but they are the same.

THAT WINTER

Refugees tread meadow roads
with the loud rustling of endless grief.
    "Night Is a Cistern," ADAM ZAGAJEWSKI

The large stone house. A stone barn.
Two chimneys on the house.
Window shades closed except for a few on the second floor.
There was a narrow road up to the house.
The weeds beside the road clumped with snow.
Scrub trees between more outbuildings raised accusatory limbs.

A wagon lumbered across the matted weeds. A travois hopped.
The small band of Indians passed—
A bird flew from the tree as they continued through the furrows.
The people watched from the windows of the large stone house.

FIELDNOTE

They gave me a rock
brown with a trace of snow or a few clouds above a field.
A small opening in the middle like a beak or the blade of a tiny plow.

I am in my car. I pass a row of pine trees. A farmhouse in the distance.
I am behind a car now.
A windshield wiper on the back window works in slow motion.

But what of the small brown rock they gave me?
300 million years old, they said.

Rock from Middle English *rokke*.
Old English *roke*.
Old German *rocko*.

Maybe the driver doesn't know how to turn the wiper off.
Maybe he is preoccupied. Or stoked on travel and unaware of it.

When I first had my car I didn't know how to stop the wiper from waving
at the back window.
Maybe the driver is asking for help.
For someone to stop him, hold him in their arms.

They gave me a rock for my journey so I would have company.
There are voices in a rock.
A song from a beak or a plow's rip in the soil for crops.

In winter the pines have their sleeves of needles.
The clouds heavy and gray.
The rock they gave me marked with snow.

UPDRAFT

They can indeed not be careful that they were thankful
That they should distinguish which and whenever—
    Part II, Stanza III, *Stanzas in Meditation*
    GERTRUDE STEIN

Vaquero Shelter, Seminole Canyon State Park, Val Verde County, Texas—

The Spaniards brought the church over the sea which medieval maps showed upside down on the underside of the world whenever they sought that which they didn't know.

Christ was the inhabitant of the church which the Spaniards brought whenever they expanded the world— now west— then north across the Rio Grande which they found whenever they would arrive.

The Spaniards were hot in their metal helmets and vests. The sky was copper whenever the wind blew dust in the air which was from their horses whenever they chased Indians running to the canyon.

On the cliff wall which the Indians drew— a red box for a church— the cross with tiny spines as if agave or one of those spikey feather grasses. A hairy cross. Whenever the wind blew and lifted the skirt of the church— they saw the feet they drew there.

Fearing the soldiers would come with weapons to cut off another foot which Christ needed whenever he walked. Or he was still on his cross which they carried whenever they came with his eyes nearly rolling from his head.

Painted in red after the arrival of the Spaniards,
the church and figures are part of the Pecos
Canyon rock art along the Rio Grande, Big Bend
National Park, Texas.

SEVERANCE

I have lived between places.
Having nowhere but a journey on the land. Displaced into displacement.
A verb becomes an object. Motion is destination.
I am not the same in different places. The world is floating loose.
There is barren ground. Tossing wind.
At night the quarter moon flat as a whitewall tire.

ALPHABET

AMONG MY FRIENDS ARE LETTERS
OF THE ALPHABET

They will add any word at most.
Part IV, Stanza XXIV, *Stanzas in Meditation*
GERTRUDE STEIN

As a loner I write a lot as I have to have something to do and the letters of the alphabet always are there. I need them because I live near a barren wilderness I am afraid will swallow me if I don't occupy myself and writing seems to fill that desperate need.

I can't read your handwriting is a sentence I have heard frequently though I try to pry open the letter e that always closes like an i without a dot above it, or an eye that seems to close in the long afternoons like roly-polies or the 4 o'clocks in your mother's yard she wouldn't share with you, being a loner herself and not willing to share house or yard or self as you were growing up 70 years ago.

I had a brother but he too seemed inaccessible. Living on his island off the coast that was our house wherever we lived, in which whoever came would enter after drowning, and is why our father was not eager except on the occasion of his birthday when we held an austere celebration for him with cake.

My family was the front seat in an old car. In those days, the seat wouldn't move forward or recline. The car had a clutch and gear shift and a knob on the steering wheel with which to turn as it went down the street and ahead was a corner.

The hood ornament was a figurehead on the bow.

Tires always seemed underinflated and made a clomping sound over the pavement as if galloping. And curb feelers helped you park by the curb without scuffing the white walls.

Near the houses where we lived was a vacant lot and a convent though I wasn't Catholic but Methodist though both believed Jesus was Savior though he remained on the cross in the Catholic Church and in the Methodist Church he was gone. And it was our duty to tell others of Jesus. And when I heard from a friend that a friend we both knew had died, I thought I heard her, upon seeing Jesus in death, say, why didn't you tell me, and I said I thought I did, and she said I couldn't read your handwriting.

Sometimes I add letters to words. As an e to whom as in whome because then I see home for which I always am looking. And have looked for in all the years of my living. The w was the front porch which houses had in those days with a swing for sitting outside. And in the moveable, mergeable world in which I lived, the w also was the picket fence around the yard. Or the barrier reef against the wilderness. In nightmares I never could tell if I was on land or sea.

Often I make a noun a verb as my room homes my pencils and paper and erasers. And as I write a lot I also sharpen my pencils a lot. With the jagged noise that sounds like trying to start a car with its engine already running.

On the subject of cars. They also have been friends. On the subject of pencils. They have been the cause of friends, which are the letters of the alphabet that make words.

Outside the front porch and the fence that surrounded the home was the barren wilderness. It was the state of dependence and pupilage. As trees of the woods are helpless and can be cut down. As leaves are dependent on the helpless trees. The wilderness was full of insects, squirrels, rabbits, opossum, racoons, whales, oysters, the neighbor's dog snarling. And nightmares. All of which often I had. Nothing calmed me but the thought of writing in which I made whome.

In the fifth and sixth grades I lived in Indianapolis. Across the street, behind the row of houses, a large vacant lot held water after a storm. I walked there in my galoshes with a stick digging in the dead leaves, the roots and undergrowth.

My father was transferred several times when I was growing up. It was the 1950s when the suburbs were developing. There always was a vacant lot near our house wherever we lived, with trees and bushes overgrown with vines and an opening somewhere in the copse.

I was in Indianapolis again, August 3, 2020, driving west through the tail of a storm. I had been in Worcester, Massachusetts, at the American Antiquarian Society for a month's fellowship and was returning to Kansas. I-70 passes the south edge of downtown Indianapolis. There was road construction, narrow, shifting lanes bordered with construction barrels, large transport trucks passing cars that usually passed them. It was raining hard. There was water and sticks of some sort along the edge of the road as if broken letters of the alphabet. My windshield wipers were working as fast as they could. Traffic on the eastbound lanes was stopped, but the westbound kept moving. The sky felt right above me.

I-65 joins I-70 east of Indianapolis. All I could see in the rain was road markers for I-65. I thought I had made a wrong turn and where could I turn around and get back to I-70 in the stopped traffic? I have known the feeling of desperation as a child. I was in the airburst of a storm with no direction but inward. But soon I saw the buildings of downtown Indianapolis and knew I was still on I-70 and had not made a wrong turn after all. Ahead was the junction of I-65 and I-70 where I-65 turned south and I continued west on I-70.

Later on the interstate, I saw electric-company trucks driving toward Indianapolis to repair downed lines. Later online I saw 26,000 were without electricity. I kept driving while in the rearview mirror the past continued to retreat from the car.

LEARNING THE LETTERS AT INDIAN BOARDING SCHOOL

For the United States Indian Industrial Training School,
opened 1884, currently Haskell Indian Nations University,
Lawrence, Kansas

L makes a turn like my leg and foot.
"Letters of the Alphabet," BUDD POWELL MAHAN

Writing letters of the alphabet corralled the stars. It is knowledge that
passed among them.
The letters were not an end in themselves but were parts to be used.
A letter could be placed in many words.
Its sound changed as it aligned with other letters.
The way dreams went on a journey in the night from the encampment of
their tribe.

A is for tepee.
B the buffalo with a hump on its back.
C the coyote's howl.
D a pool of light.
E is for the broken branches of the tree by the creek.
F the scrub brush, the pitchfork, the hoe.
G the glass brought by wagon for the broken window.
H the straight arms of the plough.
I is the ice in the water bucket at the well.
J for the pump-handle pumping.
K is for kick.
L a tomahawk upside down.
M is the foot of the moon on the night.

N the north wind that moans in the windows of the school.
O is an open mouth.
P a pinto pony.
Q is the coyote with its tongue hanging out.
R is the rifle the headmaster has.
S from the boys who snivel at night.
T is the starch in a Sunday collar.
U is a horseshoe in the blacksmith's fire.
V the large bird that swoops on its prey.
W is the hollow on the edge of the land.
X the log split by a hatchet.
Y is the yelp of thunder.
Z the crooked lightning.

FIELDNOTE

I step across the precarious tracts of history across the land.
The barn in the distance. The herds scattered on the land.
Air and land and space and place collaged in a Mark Rothko blaze of
blue turning to blue. #17 in particular— the cobalt, royal, and azure
bleeding into one another as rain falling from distant clouds on the
horizon.

I was reading "The Archi-texture of the City as a Network of
Translation," Chris Campanioni, *American Poetry Review*, November/
December 2020, Vol. 49/No. 6, as he reviews Brent Armendinger's
"The Operating System"—

> I have taken so many 'field notes'…a mobile text that re-
> members itself upon every peregrination, becoming a
> polyphonic, meta-textual archive—

Armendinger has traveled the land, I thought. He has the language of the spatial, "the networks of phatic communion." He talks about traces, visages, and I see the plainness, the tribes that roamed and warred.

November 14, 2021— I didn't know at first my new car had a retractable roof— but when I did, I opened it when I slept in a rest area returning to Texas on I-10 from Los Angeles— at the far end of the lot where it was dark— I lay in the back of the car and watched the sky. I saw a falling star but could not wish. All I wanted was the night to myself with the stars standing over me.

A LINE, AN X, ANOTHER LINE

An investigation of Europe's cave art has revealed shapes that
could be the world's oldest code—
   "Code Hidden in Stone Age Art May Be the Root of
   Human Writing"—
   New Scientist, November 9, 2016
   ALISON GEORGE

It was a while before they noticed the marks recurring on the walls—
bison, horse and animals of indeterminate kind.

Italy, Spain, Portugal, France.
Dots, lines, triangles, squares, zigzags, ladder and feather shapes.
They were abstract lines no other animal could make.

Were they warnings of enemy tribes? Did they mark migration trails?
Were they directions to a field of berries?
Were they observations of the clouds before a storm?
Or the bright wind ruffling leaves?
Were they an endearment?— Nothing was the same after others left?

Those rudimentary marks of one thing standing for another could
record the beginning of awareness of surroundings.
The act of consciousness. Of consequence. Of reason.

The first writing was thought to be the 5,000-year-old cuneiform script
of Uruk [now known as Warka, Iraq].
But the symbols spread on cave walls along trade routes maybe 40,000
years ago.

Were they a deliberate, repeated sequence of marks? Or random?

The marks could be tallies of a hunt. Or rationing in a time of hunger.
An X between two lines could mean shelter after a day's journey.
Or a place for crossing the river.

Possibly the marks began the process of writing— maybe copying a leaf
or a coiling tendril.
Or rain falling at the mouth of the cave.
Nothing for sure— but guessed to be formation of the long journey
from scribble.

THE INVENTION OF LOSS

There was a longing of words to belong to one another—
to move beyond what could be said.
This begins in a ripping of words. The sound of paper tearing.
Of trying again.

Later that day we walked along the dry creek bed.
We crossed into the pasture.
There was a tree line to the south. Another to the east. Gnarled.
Scruffy. The words longed to get at the essence beneath what they said.
They wanted to act nonrepresentational.
They wanted to react to a moment of wanting to hold together in all the
undoing that living is.
To call to a purpose beyond.
Faith is an interpreted world.
The aridity of summer.
The dry cold of winter on the southern plains.
Snowstorms fall, but do not want to stay.

The horse eats grass in his pasture all day,
and of an evening gets sweet feed in his bowl.
Usually a leaf has fallen into it from the tree under which he waits.
I tell him he can eat leaves. By faith, he will be full.
He waits until I bring him sweet feed in the bucket.
He has a line of trees along the dry creek bed to stand under.
An open shed for shelter.
Faith is constructed in the barren field.
A turning of pages.
The foliage of writing surrounding it.

The shed for the horse has three sides. The fourth left open to the south.
The nothingness is everywhere.
Sometimes I call out to whoever is there.
Whomever. Whomever. I say on purpose.

What do I get from the field? Assurance. A peculiar word.
I enter a territory somewhat undiscovered, yet right here among us.
Sometimes the horse follows.
I can look at my shortcoming, and find a covering in the blood of Christ.
Not every Christian has the same interpretation I do.
Not every Christian seems to have the same rock.
In fact, there are many pages in Christianity. I go to prepare a book
for you.

In my house are many territories. Within the territories there are other
territories.
No man comes to the Father of territories but by me— John 14:6.
It is the territory, the terrain, the country, the wilderness marked by Christ.
He was in the wilderness with the wild beasts— Mark 1:13. Yet they
tore him not. He is the Savior who died for the world, for his believers,
his flock. His flood.
I was taken to church as a child.
I have continued in church through my long life.

I hear children down the road playing in the leaves.
I hear them call as the leaves fly over them and fall around their ears.
There is a sanctuary. A refuge for the leaves.
A refuge from the storm that blows them across the yard.
A fortress in the wilderness. More hurtful than I can defend.
I am open to the elements. Yet I have been spared.
My shade from the sun. My light from the darkness.

UNBOUND

old place   they came from   those living here
Interview with Wilbur Sequoyah
Cherokee Narratives: A Linguistic Study
DURBIN FEELING

In 1838 the Georgia militia gathered the Cherokee in stockades,
then marched them west.
They threw the metal letter plates of the Cherokee syllabary
from the newspaper office, *The Phoenix*, into the dirt.
The letters had printed editorials against the Indian Removal Act of 1830.
They printed words— encroachment, harassment, burnings.

The letters torn apart, stomped in the dirt, broken by horses' hooves,
were stunned at first.
What was this that was not ink that rolled across their bellies?
It was the dirt— this new ink.
It was soil.
The letters were no longer in stalls of the printer's drawer—
no longer held in a yoke on the press.
They were— what was the word— mobile?— ambulatory?

The letters dug in the dirt.
They romped.
They followed the roots of trees.
They crawled across the ground.
Wind loosened them— carried their spirits— their intent.
The letters spoke to the air.
The birds answered.

The letters continued into creeks and rivers.
They spoke to the fish.
They spoke to the animals.
They wore fins and tails and ears. The letters went into the fields.
They became plows.

The letters followed the people on the Removal Trail.
They came to the New Territory.
The Cherokee *Phoenix* was printed again in 1844.
It was in breaking apart— coming back together,
the letters formed new ways to speak.
How to start again from nothing.
How to cut trees and build cabins.
How to plant crops. How to write laws.

The letters had been on a long journey.
They saw the movement of the constellations at night.
They watched lights move slowly across the sky.
Language was a keeper of memory.
It belonged to the earth.
Now it belonged also to the stars.

BUT ALSO OF THOUGHT

MOLTEN GLASS POURED ON DECOMPOSING FEATHERS INSIDE A ROUND MOLD

Pheasant Wing Remains Within Glass 4
LIZ MARKUM
2020
Glass, copper, bone, ash, sand, 10 x 10 x 5"
University of North Texas CoLAB, Denton, Texas

For Kamloops and Marieval where the bones of Native
children have been found— and for others to come—

They are digging in a field.
A Native residential school or sanitorium for the undoing of structure.

What remains but a line, 2 dots, and the slightest smudge of feathers—
a remnant of flight.

They are digging in a field.

Maybe they will find an ax, a pick. A nickel from a giant's pocket.
An idea for re-structure.

The sight of clouds behind the moon transparent as a wing
inside the circle of the glass.

IN THE BEGINNING: THE IMPORTANCE OF WILDLIFE IN THE DEVELOPMENT OF HUMAN THOUGHT

Sometimes it is possible to say more with broken structure than it is with straightforward text.

I wanted a causeway in coastal thought that has nothing to do with wetlands, but rather with the historic Cherokee woodlands and the Biblical Book of Genesis.

How naming animals caused what may have been a first act of poetics.

A creative attempt to create the use of animals in creating creative thinking.

Animal from the Latin *animalis,* having breath, living being. Meaning acknowledgment for its *being.*

And finally, how the animal and the word join in the act of nomenclature.

> Could-be animals. Unexplained weather. Maybe they see us
> that way. Knowing better, the closer they get.
> "Driving at Night," RIO CORTEZ

Or maybe we know them better once they've been named and shaped by the word. The word and the animal as one.

A historical perspective—

Early, the Cherokee were evangelized and assimilated. They thought it would save them from removal from their land.

The Cherokee were a Woodland tribe with an abundance of animals in the woods. Deer. Elk. Bear. Wolf. Fox. Turkey. Rabbit. Squirrel.

There was meat. Hides for shelter and clothing. Hides for trading.

Early, the Cherokee took the ways of the European. They had cattle, pigs, chickens on their farms.

The European wanted deer hides. The Cherokee supplied them— until realizing there were fewer deer to hunt. They traded for metal pots and instruments. They traded for calico for dresses and fabric for men's turbans.

The word "deer" comes from the Middle English *deere, dere, der, dier, deor*, small animal. From the Old English *deor*, animal. Proto-West Germanic *deur*. Proto-Germanic *deuza*. Proto-Indo-European *d^{h}ewsom*, meaning living thing, from *d^{h}ews*, breath.

The cougar and owl also were acknowledged— because they were nocturnal. They were watchmen. Keepers of the woods until daylight would claim itself as watchman again.

Dogs were pack and food animals. The word "dog" comes from the Old English *docga*. Its origin is unknown. It was picked up in other languages. French *dogue*. Danish *dogge*. German *dogge*. Spanish *perro*, origin also unknown. Old Church Slavic *pisu*. Polish *pies*. Serbo-Croatian *pas*.

It is words that inhabit our language. As many words as animals in the woods—

[The compilation of Cherokee explanation tales by James Mooney— "The Girl Who Married an Owl." The story of the turtle's segmented shell and how it was sewn back together— as if quilt-work. Stories of how the squirrel stretched its skin and became a flying squirrel that saved someone from harm. The Possum and the Terrapin who went out to hunt persimmons. The use of the wolf's ears for hominy spoons.]

First Act of Wildlife Management: Naming—

Genesis 2:19, out of the ground the Lord God formed every beast of the field, and every fowl of the air and brought them unto Adam to see what he would call them: and whatsoever Adam called every living creature, that was the name thereof.

In Biblical tradition, it was animals that provided a useful use of language. The fundamental act of naming. A port for the imagination.

The earth is 4.543 billion years old. There were past encampments of life. Unknown except for what we know from fossils and bone fragments and evidences in rock formations.

But as for the beginning of our present encampment— after the void the earth was in again in Genesis 1:2— we begin with a new beginning in the Book of Genesis.

There had been men before Adam who could split a stone and tie it to a stick for a weapon and eventually sharpen the stone and tie it to the stick for a spear. But as for Adam— according to the Bible— God formed man from dust and breathed his breath into him.

He named man and woman but left the animals nameless. A horrific act— not to be named. But left the naming to Adam as a stronghold against the void.

Cattle, fowl, every beast of the earth— How did God bring them before Adam? Was it one by one? How long did Adam observe the animal? Did he consider its characteristics? What to name one animal in contrast to another? How did he remember the names he had named? Was someone taking notes? If so, what did they write on? What did the writing look like?— a clutter of twigs after a storm?

In Native stories, the imagination continued past naming and reliance upon.

In "Two Dogs in One" from *Cherokee Narratives: A Linguistic Study, Recovering Language and Literacies of the Americas Initiative,* University of Oklahoma Press, 2018, the authors, Durbin Feeling, William Pulte and Gregory Pulte tell stories without grammar and the standard subject / verb / object construct of the English language—

They are stories transcribed from the Cherokee, such the story about a dog who walked home one night both with a boy and the boy's parents and brother after they visited a neighbor who had television. The boy started home first. The parents and younger brother stayed behind talking to the people. How could one dog be in two places?

Two Dogs in One

a few years when it was I just a boy yet when it was we liked
it was television for us to watch it but not also we ourselves
we didn't have television and not also electricity even we
didn't have where we lived house however near we apart they
had television and not also really near not close to each other
somewhere I suppose one mile distant they lived at a distance
however we would go for us to watch television approximately
ten half time until we would go there and return news after the
telling of until and that what we had thought it was one time
we went father mother brother and I and my sister who is yet
Washington operation schools that place she lived there and
that the reason not she was not with us and dog also brown
we had good hunter and also house watcher and obedient stay
when you tell him he would stay and also if we took him with
us he would go it was and that dog he followed us when we
went and when we arrived there at their home and just there
outside toward the porch he lay down he waited for us as we
returned until and at that time then as we got ready to upon
our return as we got up all and the door toward as we walked
they began again to talk father mother and others and that
again when they did he just went on out my brother and about
two minutes about ahead he started out and for ourselves

which was father and mother together then as we came out the
brown dog ours he got up outside toward porch he was lying
and that dog he joined us the distance to our home as far as
and when we returned to our home my brother already he was
home and our bedtime then we were preparing we were talking
I mentioned the dog him following us home the distance and
my brother silent he became for a while but then when he
spoke up this he said how can that be me also also the distance
he followed me

FIELDNOTE

There are places in the Bible where I see Native thought. "Thou shalt
be in league with the stones of the field"— Job 5:23 "But ask now the
beasts, and they shall teach you, and the fowls of the air, and they shall
tell you. Or speak to the earth, and it shall teach you, and the fishes of
the sea shall declare unto you"— Job 12:7.

In "Reading the Indigenous night sky to interpret wildlife patterns,"
Trevor M. Leaman, *Wildlife Australia Magazine,* 2019, says an Aboriginal
constellation is the Emu in the Sky. "It is found in the dark dust lanes of
the Milky Way between the Southern Cross (head), Scorpius-Sagittarius
(body) and Ophiuchus-Aquila (feet)." The changing orientation of the
celestial emu fits the migration and breeding patterns of the terrestrial
emu.

In the long memory of recorded time— the thought process of poetics was first among us as causeway over the unstable waters of our existence.

On FB I saw a quote by Virginia Woolf— I am writing to a rhythm and not to a plot. When I read it, I thought, I want the poetry of the plot.

Poetry has its exegesis in the unstrung. But poetry also is story.

.

TWO FIELDS, ONE TO THE EAST OF THE HOUSE, ONE TO THE SOUTH

You begin with a few words. Then other words want to join them. Words off to the side you didn't realize were there until you started. Then other words that connect to those other words are there. Back and back to the beginning. Many come to ride along. Some are carriers of the burdens. Those are the words you tell first. Then words that have nothing to do with the story begin to crowd in.

At first the story seems too small. It cannot contain everything that wants to speak. But you let all the words in. The world you speak grows large enough to contain them. Until the world grows so large it collapses. And is gone. The people. The animals. Even the stars disappear. They leave the dug graves of their black holes.

> You may not know
> how much terror we bear—
>   "Vespers," LOUISE GLUCK

Jesus asked who his mother was— Mark 3:33.

I also can ask who was mine. A person outside herself and therefore I was outside also. A woman who could not connect with a child. Who was in a place she was not comfortable. Not wanting to be there. Where I happened to be also. But it was not her choice. Nor mine either. She did what she was supposed to do. Have a child. Do her chores. And finding she was a remote road by herself. And didn't know who herself was.

She was raised on a farm. A closed-off place. The old farm-road originally did not go beyond the creek. We made long trips to her parents' farm from which she came. To the farmhouse at the end of a long, dead-end dirt road.

She lived in a realm where what others thought dictated our behavior. What we did. Who we were. Upright in the eyes of the community of the Methodist Church. And the neighbors. And those my father worked with.

There was fire that never burned in her. Except in far reaches where wild animals roamed and the fear of them kept her in the house away from the wilderness she knew was there.

It was the days when women were housewives. Purveyor of the homestead. A rifle at her side to shoot anything I said. The animals of the wilderness were not as wild as the one in the house. The mother who did not know herself. Who did not know there was a self to know. Who had to obey some unwritten law of acceptance by others.

Now on my own place. One evening. I see from the window. The sun slantwise across the earth. The late afternoon light lifts the bleached winter field to the east. The dark woods behind it stays grounded. It is not often a plain, mown hayfield receives eminence. Where mice scatter among hay-stubbles, and soon the rain, and then the summer with its heavy crop.

Mid-winter there was a fire in the far corner of the south field. It came from the field next to it. Crossing fence line. I opened the pasture gate for the brush units when they arrived. Dissuading the horse who wanted to leave. And now in late winter the new, short grasses already have turned green. While the unburnt field is still straw.

The Indians knew fire renewed the land when they lit the prairie. The new grasses brought bison and other game. Fire is transformation by death of what it consumes.

Now the morning sun lights the white horse in the south field. The lonely end of the dirt road remembered. Maybe it is my mother, in white, outlined in the field.

The voice of the story you tell is reversal. The lowly shall be lifted. The high shall be low. There is life after death, Jesus said. The transformation by fire of believing it is there. As the line of fire advanced from the field beside it.

I want to speak of the difficulty of who one is. I remember dismissal when I wanted to speak. To speak of faith is dismissal also. She died later with cancer in her bones. The road I take back to the farm to leave a kitchen-match on the edge of the field where the farmhouse used to be.

The history of Indians gone before the farm was gone. Pawnee, Osage, Kansa, Wichita among others. Before the land was harrowed into rows. A substance made of smoke rising in gray trails along flame-lines. The old farmhouse. My mother's house. My own house without her. The field in Kansas. The fields in Texas I am with now.

The same unresolved roads. Whatever I am. When I go back. All of it plowed fields. Somewhere there has to be a shallow place where the cellar was. Or the farmhouse with the sagging upstairs floor. Or the pump for the well.

I TELL MY BONES

His psalms were roaming herds. Supplication of wildlife. South Texas.

His wing feathers. Bone and sinew. Outcries.
Finally making narrative.

They pierced my hands and feet— Psalm 22:16. Parted my garments.

A line of range. He was quacking. But not duck. The sometimes close-up.
Sometimes distant God.

QUILTLINE

they were walking back their home toward church
at that time they walked and not light
however they used to it were the curves
but this time which is bushes they bumped into—
    "Little People"
     Cherokee Narratives: A Linguistic Study
     DURBIN FEELING

HORSE

For a little while   still will be stopping
  "For the Last Wolverine," JAMES DICKEY

I walk in the wet leaves to feed the horse.
The drip of rain on the metal roof
is a finger tapping a drum.
Over the fence a torn horse-blanket thrown.
The clouds not heavy enough for rain to fall steady
but leak like an old bucket
into which sweet feed is ladled,
some of the seed dripping
through a small crack in the bucket
as I walk to the horse.
Beyond the pasture
a road cuts through a field.
Beyond the field a far stretch of land
as if a sea on which disciples wait.
Because he walked on the sea
he thought we could follow.
Lord, I come to the water where you say, walk.
Just step onto the nothingness
as though it were solid.
My thoughts   still stop at you.
The trees are oars standing on their end.
The branches barren of their leaves.
A near-dark, cloudy winter evening.
Somewhere
under a dock
waves hit against the barrels.

THE GOSPEL OF MARK ENDS ABRUPTLY

Scholars believe the book ends at Mark 16:8 with Mary
Magdalene, Mary the mother of James and Salome at Jesus'
tomb. The last twelve verses are thought to have been added
by someone later.

The crucifixion was upheaval.
Then women found the tomb empty.
A man sitting there said— he is not here. He has risen.
The women fled. They trembled. They were amazed.
They were silent. They were afraid.

Here Mark stops his gospel.
Maybe intending to go on —later— when dust settled.

Quickly he had written the book—
Listening to Peter who fled prison to Mark's mother's house—
Acts 12— and talked for days the way Peter did hastily about
Jesus' life, saying, this and this, and this—
and Mark wrote— nonstop— until he stopped
and did not go on, though after death Jesus appeared
to his disciples, saying *go into the world,*
and ascending into heaven.

A road through the sycamores at night— a yard-light in the distance
Mark— if he kept writing— might have mistaken for a candle.

CANYON WALL DRAWINGS

Neither in mean nor meaning
They will be presently be spared
They will all feel all which they please
    Part V, Stanza XXXII, *Stanzas in Meditation*
GERTRUDE STEIN

Pictographs on a cliff overhang in Seminole Canyon, Val Verde County, Texas, near the Rio Grande—

The Indians migrated as they walked in large circles returning to the same places to gather roots. Nuts. Bark. The Indians migrated they walked. Gathering sotol, leadweed. Wild onion bulbs. Leaves of the agave. Grasshoppers and insects. Small reptiles. Fish. The Indians walked in large circles. They camped under the overhang of the canyon wall in a place they could be hidden and not reached from the other side of the canyon if they standing there saw. They drew pictographs of the sacred world they saw there standing. The earliest quilt-work. Where clouds were a quiltline in the distance from the canyon wall on the near side of the other world.

WALKING ON A CLOUDY NIGHT

The barn door of the clouds closed on the full moon.
Its light seen through narrow spaces between the boards of the door.
The windy night moved the barn.
The moon moved with it.
The people told stories of the light hidden in the barn.
They told stories of the moon before it was seen.
Before it was known.
How it followed the earth.
Changing places.
Changing shape.
How could a barn hold such light?
Strange as the beak of God in a womb.

BODY WITHOUT LANGUAGE

The virus made a Zoom of words. A bullfight. The images reversed by the camera. The bull with cape and sword. The matador with four feet and tail. Your left hand is your right. Is not history shown in reverse images? When wrong is right and right is wrong. The mix-up travels along the horizon. Up is still up and down is down. The people tell stories of the old ways. Their heads turn backwards when they speak. The bulls run in narrow streets followed by the men. The danger of being gored. Those parts of the stories they haven't told. The futility of the cape. Never mind the blood. The bull in his trousers and flat-bottomed slippers. His horns curled under the bulbs at the sides of his matador hat.

TROTLINE

There were men who followed him.
Disciples they were called.
When he went for a walk on the water they were rowing in a contrary
wind—
the fish nets folded beneath them.
He would have passed them— scripture says—
but he heard their call walking on the sea as if a on paved road or gravel.

He had told them to go ahead to Bethsaida or Capernaum or
Gennesaret— those places the writers of the gospels confused.
In a boat or ship or trawler on the sea or place of water.

They had fed the crowd with loaves and fishes.
He told his disciples he would catch up with them while he sent away
the people and went to a mountain to pray.
But he saw the men toiling to row for the wind was against them.

He would have passed them— Mark 6:48— but they saw him and cried
out.
How often he came as a line of lightning with hooks spread out before
the thunder called its names.

FIELDNOTE

And he went forth again to the sea.

On a Thursday evening, December 3, 2020, I began a Zoom Advent
Study from the Book of Mark with Father Spencer Reece at St. Mark's
Episcopal Church in Jackson Heights, New York.

Mark is the oldest of the four gospels. Mark, Matthew, Luke, John.
Mark must have listened to Peter talk of his time with Christ.
The first attempt to write is the hardest. Rudimentary.
Over which who knows what is there.

And they went up to the roof and broke into it and let down the bed
with the man sick with palsy— Mark 2:4.
Jesus and his disciples were sitting on the couch when the hacking began.
Maybe Jesus looked at the sick man and said, be healed.

Maybe Jesus looked at the roof and said, your sins are forgiven.

TWO SPIRALS ON THE CANYON WALL

Often it was about the sea. The merfolk and other mashups that swim for those on ships to look down in the water upon. The aberrations that don't belong. Of different parts stitched together. Columbus saw them on his voyage. Shakespeare in his imagination. Pliny the Elder who knows where he was. Sand crabs surely would eat them. Maybe octopi. The mermaids fled the Spanish Conquistadors. They left stories of geezer waves that washed onshore and left them stranded. The battering winds blowing birds from cottonwoods and mesquite. The mermaids and their side-mates. Little pieces of scales flicked off for wave lines on the water of the Gulf.

QUILTLINE

For Shawnee Indian Mission Manuel Labor Boarding School,
1839-1862, now Shawnee Mission National Historical Site, Shawnee
Mission, Kansas. Annual Reports to the Commissioner of Indian Affairs
listed tribes— Chippewa, Delaware, Fox, Iowa, Kansa, Kickapoo, Miami,
Munsee, Osage, Ottawa, Peoria, Potawatomi, Quapaw, Sauk, Shawnee,
Stockbridge, Wea and Wyandot.
With description of the manual labor the Indian students performed.
Denominations that provided support— Baptists, Catholics,
Methodists, Moravians, Presbyterians and Quakers.

It was there since the earliest days.
The transfigurement of pastel robes of the disciples the sun
shone through.
As if a clothesline of stained-glass windows.
A quiltline.
The horizon of land and sky where I lived. The crops in the field.
The animals in the pasture.
The enormous emptiness to be transformed. The dearth of invisibility.   81
Yet the stone rolled away.
The linen clothes folded in the empty tomb.
The napkin around his head wrapped in a place by itself— John 20:6-7.

PSALMS

Unless the Lord had been my help, my soul had
almost dwelt in silence—
    Psalm 94:17

HISSING IN THE LEAVES

Though you have broken us in the place of dragons—
Psalm 44:19

At the beginning I made note of the world I knew.
The words had nothing to do with one another.
Once I had a Big Chief Tablet. Geranium red.
Pungent.
I pushed the tablet to my nose.
Across the field.
The tossing trees.
The dragons howling from the wilderness.

Now I hold the paper on my lap.
I write words with a pencil.
There is a yellow light behind the tree line across the field.
Muted as dust behind a mower.
The field still a pool of darkness.
Later in the day the man who owns the field passes on his tractor.
Passing again with a machine that rolls the cut hay into forage for animals.
Later a wagon comes from down the road and lifts the field of its weight.

CURSIVE

A Long Trip North

The practice of handwriting. A formation of islands. Territories to be traversed. A silent wish.

Cursive from the Medieval Latin *cursivus*. From Latin *cursus*, past participle of *currere*. To run. To course.

It is the story of the earth. Movement. Momentum. The plates beneath the crust— paragraphs in opposition. The wind patterns. Currents. Animal migrations. Early people walking places they could not see— but following a journey they felt within. Later people often walking from expulsion or the need to leave a place they could no longer live. Even foliage. Its forceable removal from trees in autumn. Even roots crawl underground.

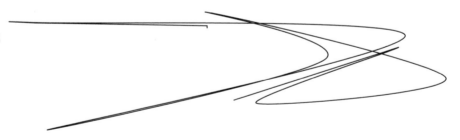

Adney Lake. Northern Minnesota. Sandy Lake. All those lakes. Staying in a cabin on Adney. Driving to others. The flat lakes with few waves in their mouth. Unbothered by boats. Late fall. Watching the handwriting of water among reeds on the edge of the lake. To course. To circle back and forth. To make motion. A blade against a cold surface.

The movement of a ship embarking across the unknown waters. Perilous. The edge of the ocean appears.

Cursive began with expulsion. The parting from letters standing separate from one another in a manuscript. Now written to be connected with loops and curtsies. To be carried. To be preserved. As the resonate history of removal.

The Indian tribes knew war. The Chippewa and Dakota fought one another before the arrival of the Europeans. They pushed out one another. They wanted hunting grounds. They wanted *place* where they felt oneness move through the trees. The Europeans landed there. Not to be removed. As a word from its sound in cursive. Onto islands overwashed with waves.

Handwriting moves like an oar. To course. To discourse. To disperse. To mark with fragments of vines. Twigs. Cattails. The entanglements of water. Placing oral stories into the silence of written words. Another expulsion they brought.

At night by campfire. The old stories shiver. A brush wolf in the distance. The call of an owl. A voice from across the lake. Water carries sound across its surface.

1850. The governor of Minnesota decided to disperse annuities for ceded land. At Sandy Lake. 258 miles west of Madeline Island. The Chippewa traveled rivers, creeks and portages. Waiting through October November December. Duped. Set up. The government officials left the Natives abandoned. Hoping they would die from hunger and exposure. The annuities only partly came. Later. On Sandy Lake. The Chippewa returned to Madeline Island across frozen creeks and rivers. They carried the bodies of children back with them.

These words I write on the page. The *scurrrrr* of a pencil on paper. The supplanting of one on another. Ripples across the shore that is my page.

The barely audible background of place.

PSALM TO WHOM(E)

I am nothing. I am nothing. Father in the volcano. Ice cap. Snowfall.
In failure and failure.
Father— To whom am I speaking? To whom I am speaking.
It is you Father to whom I come in absolute struggle to believe. To follow.
I am alone. Without distraction. Tessellate. Fretful. In distress.
Over and over.
I come before you a deflated bag.
I give you myself. What I was before I was broken.
Something maybe itself broken as it was spoken into being.
As it was being named.
For a while, there was a way out of being by not being. By being invisible within one's cage.
There were times I could not speak. An inability to show my ineptitude.
I was on a caliche plain. Arid. And. Though I could hear rain on the roof and against the window.
This is the beginning of my being, unknowable God. The words I make come from myself.
Trying the ridge of stodginess.
I thought of her this morning when my long sleeve was caught inside the
sleeve of my coat. And I worked to pull it loose.
His hunting gun no longer there.
Even he lost what he was in the strange land of responsibility for family.
An act he himself did not want to commit. But did.
This is what you do in isolation. I tell her. Though she is gone. Though she could not find.
You rake together the little barren passages.
You take the clutter of letters in the alphabet. Shuffle them back and forth.
Place one next to another and use spaces between them.
They will look at first something like Native pictographs.
They will make a home in the wilderness. They break apart and scatter.

Their messages on cave walls and on your own scattered pages cover the nothingness.
You take whatever knowledge you have and hold onto it.
You breathe your breath into it.

FIELDNOTE

Home is idea.
Home is place.
Home is memory.
Home has rooms.
Home from the Old English word, *ham*, a village where many gathered.
Home is assemblage.
Home is pasture. Horses. Dogs. Barn. Shed. House.
I want to hear the coyotes howl. I want the stars so low to the earth they kiss.
Home is sanctuary.
Home is a dirt road.
If home is idea, the roof doesn't leak.
Home is history.
Home is where the horses howl.
Home is shelter. It has hills. Trees that hold the moon in their mouth.
Home is a prom dress. With buttons missing. The hem ripped. I spread the dress on my bed. Under the ceiling light— I lie on the dress. It was an island on which I floated. I felt I drowned— though I was still breathing.
Home is the edge of a shallow field where I wade in my galoshes.
How do birds lift their bodies from the slough?
Home is cabbage stirring in the pot. Roast duck in the oven.
Home is argument.
Home is a place with a fence for horses. To keep them from running away. To keep them from ripping their prom dresses. To keep them from shooting one another in the head.

We can roast marshmallows and dream we're swallowing the moon.
Home is a place that covers our trails.
A prom dress before it is ripped.
Home is journey.
It is decision.
It is open range.
It is fenced pasture on open range.

ABLUTION

The Radical Murals of Maxo Vanka, St. Nicolas Croatian Catholic
Church, Millvale, Suburb of Pittsburgh,
on One of Those Streets That Climbed the Steep Hill
After Finding a Narrow Turn-Off on One of Them
and Entering From a Side Door

Then *whammo*— a painted figure in a long black robe wears a gas mask
and holds a scale.

Inside the church— a dark Sistine Chapel of sorts— the working class,
the suffering, the heartsick, the war-torn, the wounded, the dying, the
already-dead— depicted in large panels across the walls and ceiling.
Instead of the Sistine's heavenly, these walls are filled with the horrors
of war. It is the Sistine Chapel transfigured and reinterpreted by World
War I and II that killed an estimated 115 million military and civilians
[40 million in WWI; 75 million in WWII]. It is the Chapel transfigured
by the Great Influenza epidemic of 1918 that killed one-fifth of the
world's population. It is the struggle of the poor in a system that keeps
them bound.

On the ceiling, above the figure in the gas mask, angels bring the
resurrected Christ to his Father. Their wings in flames. Their hair
standing up in the updraft of the Holy Being entering Heaven. The trees
over which they pass have uplifted hands to keep them from falling.

On the walls, front and side altars— garish images of industrialization—
coal miners, steel mills and slag piles, a World War battlefield, the ink-
black Allegheny River at night.

Above the altar, Mary, Queen of Croatia, sits on a cloud, her legs splayed to hold the man-like but child-sized Savior of the world on her knee.

Four of Jesus' disciples posted in large chairs look at the action figures. Luke with an angel— its hands to its face— its upstretched wings umbrellaed over its head.

Mark with a lion. Matthew with a winged bull. John with an eagle. Nearby another angel frowning.

In the background, factories with their appendages of chutes, ramps, smoke- stacks— as if huge octopi emitting black smoke.

The Methodist Church where I went as a child was made of Missouri limestone. The walls were plain. In the pew, I sat next to my father of the river bottoms. Of the Armour stockyards. The man who brought us meat wrapped in butcher paper that looked like my white patent-leather Sunday shoes. Blood ran from the edges of the paper when he unwrapped the meat my mother would cook for supper. An animal had died on the killing floor. It died that we might live. The cows of the field gave themselves for us. It was what Christ had done— the butcher-string that held us together.

It was my father at the summit of my going. Always my father, my Maxo Vanka, who painted my world. I was the bare walls of his church. He painted a mural of the world upon me. Instead of a paint brush he had a cattle prod. I understood the world was driven by it, and from it, he protected me.

On one of the walls— a mural, *Immigrant Mother Raises Her Sons for American Industry*— a man in a large casket on fine Croatian lace. In another mural, the body of another man on the open pages of a newspaper, his work hammer and lunch pail at his side. Smokestacks erupt as if volcanoes. At the top of the hill— a church— Ablution from the Latin *abluere*, meaning to wash away. From the prefix *ab* [away, off] and *lavere* [to wash].

In *Pieta*, Mary wears the black habit of a nun. A nimbus around her head. The rotary blades of swords at her shoulders. Two angels in green robes behind her. One stands on the sun. The other on the moon— holding a flat, prickly cactus as if a green tortilla crowned with thorns.

Maxo Vanka, a Croatian immigrant, painted murals on the walls and ceiling of St. Nicolas in 1937 and 1941-42. Tattooed it, actually, from head to foot.

Nothing sedate in St. Nicolas Croatian Catholic Church. Nothing understated. But blousy with overstatement. The whole church— its walls, ceilings, front and side altars, were drawn with figures in forest green, root beer brown, Christ-blood red.

The common people of the congregate were not inept in all this flowering of religious iconography stating that religion is anything but ordinary. They had been caught in the mouth of industrialization. Bitter with promise turned to disappointment. Horrific circumstances. Enduring poverty. Receiving the bodies of sons returned from the factories, the mines, and from war.

Endurance without question in this sacred, bizarre wrap of murals.

In *Mary on the Battlefield*, her bare foot on a soldier's chest. In one hand a bayonet. A knife in the other.

Nearby, Christ nailed to the cross. The nails more like spikes that hold his body in place. His beating heart visible. His side pierced by a soldier wearing a WWI helmet.

Father, you come to me wearing your white packing-house coat. You always return.

My brother and I cut cows from the butcher paper my father brought from the packing house. But the red crayon wouldn't mark the waxy paper.

Somewhere on a wall, a strike-line forms.

Near the altar, a rough steel worker holds the church in his hands. A Catholic priest on his knees prays for the workers. The great labor force underway. Steel workers realizing their right to organize. Priests joining strikers on local picket lines. Another angel with a flame on its forehead flies overhead.

My father faced strike-lines too in the stockyards when he moved from labor to plant superintendent. He loaded trucks when the workers would not.

I have found the walls of the Protestant Church boring. The sloggy hymns. The long sermons. The plainness. The draftiness. The sameness. Waiting for the service to be over. Many mountains remaining unmoved. Yet somewhere in the middle of it— a pit in which was salvation. A belief in Christ's atonement for the slugfest of the world. For my own inner forestation. The need for ablution.

The small St. Nicolas Church as if it had been pushed against the side of the steep hill to keep it from falling.

An invisible glob of adhesive somehow held it there.

95

https://vankamurals.org/vanka-murals/

Footnote

In 1921, there was a fire in St. Nicolas Catholic Church. The rebuilt
church remained unadorned for 16 years, until Father Zagar, a
progressive Franciscan priest, looked in the Croatian community for
someone to decorate his church with murals. It was Maxo Vanka
who saw the brutal German invasion of Belgium when he was 24.
Vanka saw the gas warfare, the blood and gore of Hitler's invasion
of Yugoslavia and Russia. He was an art professor in Zagreb with a
peasant background. He left Croatia threatened by Fascism. In America,
he painted the Depression poor and hungry. In 1935, Vanka visited
Pittsburgh and had an exhibit. There he met Father Zagar of St. Nicolas
Croatian Church.

IN COLDEST WEATHER

The horse tank is frozen.
The horse wears his horse coat.
He does not like.

He wants to drink water.
The horse waits at his horse tank.
His water is frozen.

There have been squirrels in his horse tank.
They have drowned in hot weather.
They only wanted a drink of water.

A man walks to the horse tank. He carries a sledgehammer.
The horse shall not want.

The man hits the lid of ice on the horse tank.
He hits and hits again.
The horse is not afraid.

Lord break the ice on my horse trough.
Those collected thoughts that separate me from water.
Lord of mercy.

Lord of strength and judgment.
A rusted shovel leans against the pasture fence.
It has lifted drowned squirrels from the horse tank.

Now it lifts ice chunks.
So the horse can drink water in his horse tank.
So a horse can drink the coldest weather.

THE PSALMS ON AIR MOVING

The Lord is my rock— Psalm 18:2

Under which there was a treaty. Broken. Ruffled. With pages blowing.

The Spanish intent to subjugate, Christianize, civilize the Indian—
Comanche, Keechi, Waco, Caddo, Anadarko, Ioni, Delaware, Shawnee,
Cherokee, Lipan, Tawakoni.

Another stop on another long trip. Tehuacana Creek in the Republic of Texas.

Warm night spent. The ghost of a mission bell misfiring.

It is to whom. The settlement of church attendance. The custom of.

Not forgotten. Lighter than the eaves of an old stone house.

FIELDNOTE

The plurality of reality. I was reading Pliny's *Natural History* for another
project and found the line, "this pluralitie of worlds" in his Second
Booke. This was the Philemon Holland translation published in 1634.
Poetry itself is memory. It comes from a long tradition going back to
the origin of poetry as *breath*, as root cause of being— meaning those
who are rooted in struggling with the root-cause of meaning. The root
of breath actually is the first cry in the form of a question.

There is a principle of physics working within poetry— whatever it is. Something that can't be explained because it resists capture. Like the unifying principle that physicists are looking for. There are opposing forces in the universe. The constancy principle and the theory of relativity. In poetry there is certainty and uncertainty side by side.

I don't think I can write a straight line of anything. I want the sidebar— I wanted to follow the daydream that the teacher's voice engendered. I hear it in Gertrude Stein's *Stanzas in Meditation* and Durbin Feeling's work on Cherokee linguistics. It is the way I wish I could have written in school. When I'm at my computer, it's the old road I follow back to the point along the clash-line of English and the old language I have left as a visage in my head.

One of poetry's purposes is the formation of *visage*. To substantiate the great air pocket over which we reside. Or in which we reside. The great uncertainty sucks visages toward itself. It provides a sense of certainty or substance in the likeness of certainty. The great unknown would eat us otherwise— if we didn't construct netting into which we catch something other than what is prose.

JOHN THE BAPTIST AND THE CRITICAL WORK OF WRITING WITH SCAFFOLDING LEFT IN PLACE DESCRIBING THREE INTRUSIONS OF PERSONAL ADDRESS

JOHN THE BAPTIST

JOHN THE BAPTIST I

In my own country I'm in a distant land—
   Ballade [I die of thirst beside the fountain]

He's beaten so much he reverts to form—
   Ballade [The goat scratches so much it can't sleep]
   FRANÇOIS VILLON [1431-1489]

He ate wild honey and locust. Bee stings on his face and hands. The
beating sun of day. The howling wilderness at night. Where did he get
the camel's hair he girded with a leather belt?— from traders passing
on a wilderness road? In Pieter Bruegel the Elder's *The Preaching of St.
John the Baptist*, 1566— John preaches baptism and repentance to the
crowd— the Jordan River off to the side. John baptizes with water, but
he— whose shoelaces he is not worthy to unloose— baptizes with fire.
It angers a woman who would remember his rebuke and call for his
head on a charger. Is this the religion that lasts? Not one made of one's
own desire. But called to lose one's self. Even cousin Jesus does not visit
John in prison before John's death. His disciples tell him when John is
beheaded. What faith is this?— full of peril. Betrayal. There was a man
sent from God whose name was John— John 1:6. He is not the Light,
but was sent to bear witness of the Light. A wild man who talks to
ravens. Who speaks to stones.

INTRUSION [DEFINING THE MEDIUM]

It was the crowd that filled the canvas in Bruegel's The Preaching of *St.
John the Baptist* that informed the block form of the first installation.
Of the following installation, I would say it's the ragged edge of trees in
the painting—

JOHN THE BAPTIST II

John the Baptist traveled as if a decision. A choice.
In art class the desert raked his paper.
The growing edge of new thought
not full of laws and rules
but going where it would.
What was he preaching?
Washing in the river was more than a dunk in the water.
It was the counted-on beginning.
Meaning—
A mystery of knowing. A tack. A need.
The religion that separated the world. Turned it upside down.
Jesus was coming to fill the museum.
To dominate somewhat.
John told the crowd to believe— to step into the unknown.
O Lord be with me as I lose my head.

JOHN THE BAPTIST III

What became of the head of John the Baptist is hard to determine—
[Wikipedia]. Some say it is in the fortress of Machaerus. Others say
it was taken to the Mount of Olives where it was twice buried and
discovered, giving rise to the feast of the First and Second Finding
of the Head of St. John the Baptist. Still others say, it was interred in
Herod's Palace at Jerusalem and found during the reign of Constantine
I, and taken to Emesa where it remained unknown for years, until it

was manifested by revelation in 451. An event celebrated as the Third Finding [also Wikipedia]. Different fragments of John's skull are said to be in the San Silvestro in Capite in Rome. The Amiens Cathedral in France. The Residenz Museum in Munich. And the hand with which John baptized Jesus is in Istanbul. Mount Athos. West Bengal. The bone of one of John the Baptist's left fingers is at the Nelson-Atkins Museum of Art in Kansas City, Missouri, where I went as a child for art lessons, never knowing it was there. Not privy to the inner chamber. He was nonetheless a part. The outer rim. Not belonging to the center. All that time in the desert— the narrowing of light as the sun turned away on summer evenings and locusts rubbed their legs together with a screech.

INTRUSION [PULLING THE RUG OUT FROM UNDER]

I thought as a child at the museum they would not come. Or if they did it would be late of an evening. Nearly dark as the ship passed under Crete— Acts 27:7. Not commodious in winter— Acts 27:12.

On the walk of the museum a dead locust. A cicada actually looking like an old Hudson in the salvage yard. Its squat silver body. Belly-up. Its legs in the air— shoelaces I was not worthy to untie.

I felt as a child no one could get there soon enough or would not get there at all.

Locusts are more like grasshoppers. Their legs are springs that jump them forward. A sporty Studebaker a neighbor later drove with antennae and curb feelers I could not untie.

And when the ship was caught— Acts 27:15— we let her drive. A Territory of my own defending.

JOHN THE BAPTIST IV

September 3, 2021— I went to the Nelson-Atkins Museum of Art to see the finger of John the Baptist in a reliquary— a bone in a glass cylinder— a human hand bone from Guelph Medieval Arts Brunswick Cathedral in Germany.

Did they dismantle and divide his bones? In ordinary trade? Wrist-bone finger-bone foot-bone. A game of pick-up sticks. The museum still as the absence of cicadas.

At art lessons we walked through the museum. *The Beheading of St. John the Baptist*, Hendrick ter Brugghen, Northern Netherlands 1620— there on the platter.

If you stay with the ship— Acts 27:31. After the first and second finding of the head.

INTRUSION OF ANOTHER FINDING

Across the hall in the art museum from the room where Brugghen's *The Beheading of St. John the Baptist* hung— a huge cast bronze of Max Ernst. I could see at the same time. The man's head was removed and replaced with the head of a bull. A spear in his hand. His narrow wife a mermaid. A little goat between them. A family portrait— Ernst's *Capricorn* 1948-1964. Originally cement and scrap iron. On the museum walk late summer— another cicada— a dirigible. Its transparent wing like a small clip of cellophane— not dissolving on the tongue. There were incongruities for trade. A pelt of animal hide— a hive. I traded for the world that belonged to Jesus, whom I could not see. But thought was there. Or at least there was good chance he was— for the answered prayers— for the exile of one from this world— for the distant land of his.

DUBBING

Now when John heard in prison the works of Christ, he sent
two of his disciples— Matthew 11:2

When it was late he thought. Doubted actually. Are you the one that
should come, or do we look for another?— Matthew 11:3.

John the forerunner of Christ did not know? Had the dot and tittle not
traversed his composition? It was all he had. And sent to ask assurance.
With moonlight through the prison bars bent between his fingers.

Jesus said tell John the blind receive their sight. The lame walk. The
lepers are cleaned. The deaf hear. The dead are raised. The poor have
the gospel preached to them. What more did he want?

At one time John heard the heavens open. Saw Jesus still wet with water
of the Jordan. The dove above him. My son in whom I am well pleased—
Matthew 3:17. Great God who is and should be. Say it is as you say, even
if just not yet.

THE HORSE

The horse has a 3-acre pasture
but there is a path of matted grass from his shed
to his sweet-feed bowl in a corner of the pasture.
His horseshoes mark the bare ground where he stands to eat
like an alphabet with the letters U and C
spilled on the ground.
A woman in a headscarf walks a 2-rut road through a far pasture.
A man with a stick walks on the paved road.
The hoof prints of the horses brand the dried mud.
The horse watches the child leave on the school bus
and return in the afternoon while he waits for his sweet feed.
His ears shaped like small tepees.
They turn to the airwaves in the wind that travel the world.
The horse picks up on the suffering.
He hears the call of geese, birds, field dogs.
At night the coyotes.
All the refugees.
While in the day a gray squirrel runs along the fence line by his bowl.

QUILTING

The environment is the soul of things. Each thing has its own expression and this expression comes from outside it. Each thing is the intersection of three lines, and these three lines form the thing: a certain quantity of material, the way in which we interpret it, and the environment it's in.

The Book of Disquiet
FERNANDO PESSOA

THE DISRUPTION OF FABRIC

The substance of story is an essay of land stretched over the nothingness under the sky in Southwest Texas.

There are encampments in travel on a land not traveled readily. Not translated, but barren, unused, but for passing over.

Early in the spring, I drove from North Central Texas to Big Bend National Park— or nearly there. A trip of about 10 hours.

I camped the first night in Marathon, Texas, 70 miles north of Big Bend. A one-hotel town with a few buildings and a campground to the west. The evening was cloudy. In *The Book of Disquiet*, the Portuguese poet Fernando Pessoa mentions the melancholy of drizzle. I could hear it on the roof of my car.

The next morning, I drove south to Big Bend. Passing the Gage Hotel as I left Marathon, I remembered four figures— father, mother, sister, brother. As a girl, I had a dollhouse with furniture. Even a lamp that glowed in the dark with some sort of fluorescence. A dollhouse without a back. In which I made structure. Reading Pessoa's *form of objects*, the dollhouse was there again.

As I neared Big Bend, the plain land became more ornate. Along the highway in Big Bend, there were road signs with information on the geological formations in the distance. Ouachita Fold Belt— 275-290 million years old—

Highly deformed rocks in the Ouachita Fold Belt, a northeasterly trending range, uplifted about 275 million years ago. The intricate folding is shown by whitish rock bands called caballos (the Spanish word for horses) exposed on both sides of this highway. The northeast trending Del Norte — Santiago range forms the southwestern skyline. The rocks of this range were deposited in a sea that covered Ouachita Fold Belt after erosion had reduced the highlands and later submergence lowered the area. Santiago Peak named for a local man who was killed by Indians and buried beneath the peak is the high flat-topped mountain to the southwest. It was once a mass of molten magma that cooled and hardened beneath the earth's surface and was uncovered by later erosion. The Del Norte — Santiago Range, uplifted and folded 40 to 60 million years ago, is not half the age of the Ouachita fold. This is a remarkable fusion of old and young mountains — and is unmatched at any other site in North America.

The drive-through of Big Bend was probably 100 miles from the entry on the north, to the exit on the southwest side of the national park.

I passed cut-off roads to camping areas, not seen from the road. Midway at Panther Junction, I took a spur road south to the Rio Grande. The final lap down to the petroglyphs along the river bluffs was rugged. I didn't think my car would make it. I turned around and drove the 20 miles back north to Panther Junction, where I took the highway west to Study Butte that left Big Bend.

I drove north toward Casa de Luna, an adobe house in the desert I had rented for three days. I like Pessoa's voice he divided among characters he found within himself— the first-person narratives he wrote for his different voices. Pessoa's voice splayed into parcels in the quilt-work of *The Book of Disquiet*. Plurality within the singular has been a point of interest.

CASA DE LUNA

The house in the desert of Southwest Texas—
In the day, I walked on the dirt road up the hill. The wind in the yucca
between its sharp blades spoke as I passed. I made note of the rock
formations in the rise and dip of the remote and distant land. The low
trees. The shrubs.

Three deer came to eat the leaves on the short trees by the house of
an evening. Then disappeared again into the valley. My iPhone did not
work at Casa de Luna. I had no dog. No weapon. I was alone. Vulnerable
to whatever prowled the moonless night— the javelina, rattlesnake,
the monstrous sky. The influx of immigrants into the country on the
southern Texas border occurred to me.

I thought I would watch the moon with its stars, but the sky was
overcast the nights I was there.

But late one night I woke and went to a window. I saw the quarter moon
through an opening in the clouds. I opened the door to the patio in the
fenced yard and stepped into the night. The Big Dipper was above me.
The edge of the Milky Way had the fluorescence of a dollhouse lamp on
the dark horizon. The whole back of the galaxy missing. The Big Dipper
belonged to a giant that lived in the sky. Who had put wheels on the
Dipper and pulled it across the sky. The stars ate one another when he   113
wasn't looking. I went back in the house and returned to bed.

The purpose of the visit to the house was to stay in a place in the
wilderness. To know the shifting fabric of objects was the moving night
of the given. An adobe house with a slanting metal roof. A few shrubs
outside the house trying to explain the moon that wasn't there.
The clouds that crossed the sky.
The wind in the yucca said.

I have one language to re-foil my words. Writing is indirect. It is the
only moon I have. It takes a while to get at. Other objects within it
change shape. It is unreliable. And therein, its great viability.

THERE WERE FISHING HOLES WHERE
THE OLD WORLD REMAINS.

At Casa de Luna, I sat at the table. I held the pencil in my hand. I made marks on the paper. The marks were words. The pencil rocked back and forth on the paper as I wrote. My pencil was a ship at sea. There was a night sky above the ship. The stars were rowboats. The stars were foliage. The night sky was a forest. There was solace. Danger. I wrote the sky clear with my words. The stars— a road on which I pulled a small, two-wheeled cart my father made. He painted it turquoise. On the road, I found a makeshift tent of branches in a small thicket. I made stories there with my words. There was a porpoise in the sea. The moon was in its belly. The moon was its belly. My words on the page were a forest. The porpoise crossed the stars. I was the bucket. The well. The fork in the road. My words bent as branches. The long handle of the two-wheeled cart in my hand was the pencil that held the bucket that was the sea. I was the foliage of the sky. The circle in the belly of the porpoise. I called to the lookout in the mast. I feared the triplicate of permission papers to sail the sea. The ship was the two-wheeled cart my father made. I told the porpoise there was no other moon to swallow.

LAITY LODGE

The fourth day I drove from Casa de Luna to Laity Lodge on the Frio River in Southwest Texas to the annual retreat of the Chrysostom Society where we read our work to one another. Where we talk about issues. Where we share stories and prayer. Though the trip took most of the day, I remained in Southwest Texas, passing open range. Cattle. Trucks with horse trailers. The Texas rodeo circuit.

Driving from the Chrysostom retreat several years ago, I passed a sign on Highway 16 between Llano and San Saba, Texas— Baby Head Cemetery. I turned around, and went back to read the road sign. Indians beheaded an infant and scattered the bones. It was revenge for encroachment on their land. I could see gravestones through the trees. The ghost-cries of the wind still moaned. The settlers retaliated in another skirmish. In a solemn valley where bluebells bloom.

LATER IN THE SPRING, I WENT TO GERMANY.

I attended an Indigenous Futurity Conference at the Europa-Universität Flensburg. I gave a talk. The conference ended with a boat ride on the Baltic Sea. A few days later I gave a reading from *A Line of Driftwood, the Ada Blackjack Story* at the University of Bonn.

Earlier in the day, I visited Weidereröffnung Bonner Münster, a Catholic cathedral from the 13th century built on the site of the graves of two martyrs, Cassius and Florentius. Little pieces of glass in the windows had been cut, placed together— not in recognizable form, but abstract artwork in glass— quilt-work— the story of a world pieced together with its absurdities.

Reason and hard realism. Yet the creative imagination makes a story from the pieces that are there. Associative yet disconnected. I use written language and the circus in its room. Alternatives. Obliterations. Writings put loss into a formative structure that can pass the loss and generate other possibilities. To feel the confines of the oppressive past. The broken pieces of variants for an alternative design from the friction of a realigned world. An oppositional world that can turn back upon itself. Whether martyrs murdered by authorities of government for their faith. Or Indigenous murdered for their lack of faith by the authorities of faith.

In this circumvented world of cross-fabrics, a merciful God took mercy on the lost and rented a butcher shop on the square because he also was a just God who had to judge the wayward world, and chose a lamb who also was his son to suffer judgment on the cross so the flock at large or those who chose to believe the questionable story would not suffer judgment. It was an invention of replacement in a little butcher shop on a backstreet that many could pass and choose not to notice.

I thought of the world as a moving place. Immigrants had come to Germany too. But on the southern border of Texas, they were overrunning. How many pebbles in a floating bowl before it goes under? How many immigrants can a country support before they overcome its ability to accommodate? Change and challenge to structures are a given. America is made of immigrants, after all. As fabric on my grandmother's quilts, I see pieces of my old pinafores, my father's pajamas, my mother's print dresses, my brother's shirts. All cut apart and joined in patterns. Not always going together.

Can a country say enough and no more? As the Christian God in his merciful heaven finally seems to say, the Christian heaven is for those who name Christ as their Savior. There is a story in Luke 16:19-31— A man dies and calls out to Father Abraham for a drink of water. Abraham tells him, between them there is a gulf he cannot cross. The man then asks to return to his brothers to tell them what the afterlife is like. Abraham answers, They have Moses and the prophets— let them hear them [Luke 16:29].

What if there are rules of entry? What if there is no illegal border crossing into the Christian heaven?

THE QUILTS

form, not function
quilt art at the carnegie, may 19 – june 16, 2022

There was the same disruption of fabric at the Carnegie Center for Art & History in New Albany, Indiana, where I stopped on my way from Texas to Columbus, Ohio, for a conference in early summer.

Hanging on the wall inside the door of the museum, was a quilt that was a dress or robe made of paper, dryer-lint, vintage textiles, natural dyes— indigo blues and grays. A spectacular one among the spectacular, surreal quilts. Quite a distance from the origin of Quilt c 1300: to stuff with wool, down, from Anglo-French *quilte*, from old French *cuilte*, *coute*, to mattress, bolster. Now sewn to disrupt the idea of comfort. To put on oneself what used to be worn by a bed.

There was a quilt made from old quilt pieces.

A quilt that was a billboard for a sideshow of circus events.

A quilt that looked like an old tin ceiling in a hardware store. A bombastic, windblown layered concept of embossed aluminum, bubble wrap, space blanket.

The silver-squared ceiling quilt was mounted on a frame from recycled wood from a child's swing set.

Indeed, the quilts in the museum were a haboob on established geometric quilt designs.

Recognition also belongs to the early surreal quilter, Gunta Stölzl. A member of the Bauhaus known for complex patterns of undulating lines. Who fled Germany during the Nazi regime. Who wanted contemporary relevance after the attempted erasure of her race. The disruptive years of war. She imagined the reshaped world in the art of her fabric-work.

I wanted to translate quilt-work into story. I wanted Pessoa's *form of objects* written in a quilt. Using existing words and concepts transformed into the surreal. I kept thinking of the disruption that invaded the alternate downturn and uplift of desperation and exuberance in the structure of the Psalms, which were to David as *The Book of Disquiet* to Pessoa. Also, the disruption in rock layers at Big Bend, and of all the earth, for that matter. I wanted a like story.

The idea of a just quilt inserted in a world where quilts don't belong—

PREPARE TO DIE

Truth is a wormy integer that can burrow into any hole. Truth is what it wants to be. It hears what it wants to hear. It sets up a lemonade stand and sells apple-whizz if it wants. Before the settlers and ongoers, truth sheltered on the open land. The hounding world is a bucket full of ghosts. A shimmering world of moonlight on the pond where Elbert jumps his truck. Frozen as the pond is. Elbert has the skid down with marginal skill, but he completes the rotation with the stars, the moon, the circling snow coming toward the windshield. The slippery world he knows is truth since the cavalry dispersed rations that were full of worms. Fricatives— the sound of wind between the door frame of the house into which the anger of the ghosts blows. Truth is not truth for everyone, but awkwardly makes its way onto the pond not conveniently frozen, but with little bumps and ridges not spotted until skated over and thrown. Watch out for Elbert's truck fishtailing under the moon. A falling star. No less hazardous. What music coming from the all-night band? It too is frozen lumpily.

Elbert called it a triple axel. How long could his truck skate behind the wheel of his longing? He was back in the bottom of the barrel. What difference? All the skaters trying to get out of the bucket— their feet with their blades in Edgy's. What a fit-fall. Twirlables— all of them. If you believe the truth they do. When would they learn to play?— but it was music to them. The truth of their efforts is acceptable in the beloved ear of their own head. In their music they look for an understanding that has to conform to their idea of truth. And withstand ideas contrary to their concept of truth they hold despite all of the blazeable words that are spoken. That night in the club. On the edge of the prairie. About to fall off. But held on by the belief in the truth that one would outlast the night.

Elbert saved his monies in a tin coffee can. Then it was gone. It had slipped across the pond as if wind blowing snow in the headlights. He looked around Edgy's to see who had money to spend. It was Edgy himself. But Edgy denied the theft. They circled with their truths and wouldn't let anyone in. Neither would they look at anything they didn't recognize as their own truth. The stars and moon told their own stories too until multiple truths twirled like ghosts on ice skates.

Truth was not a shape but a motion— a transition from one form to another. Changing from water to ice to water again. Alone on the road they remembered every accident that happened. Every driving without headlights to see who was first off the road not knowing about gullies and aberrations in the land, but driving as though the whole earth was full of roads. That's how they could have taken off and not let on they hadn't when they had. There was trouble within and without. That was the trouble. They could turn truth any way they wanted. They said Elbert buried his monies, but could not remember where. Everyone acting as if stealing was not wrong. None of them would come into Edgy's with their arms lifted over their head. They had fights and Elbert always was thrown out of the club.

It was winter and then close to spring thaw and the monies stayed disappeared. The mystery of not knowing who did the pilfering— the taking of whatever truth Elbert wanted to call stealing.

Elbert and Edgy were cousins in the relative-based community that wandered in and out of Edgy's and across frozen ponds to snuffle with colds and bad teeth and coughs and whatever else ailed them.

Edgy and The Integers, his band, played their form of music that was not music but a loud sound that defined them. It explained the pitfalls. The holes in the backroads. Everyone trying to pervert truth so they could do what they wanted and not have to obey order. The dreaded word of their world. They would go out on the pond and fight it out with their trucks. They would play dead-man-in-the-hole. Death was everyone's truth, after all. The black hole of the universe in the black hole of the pond where the ice broke under the guilty truck.

LATER

The fabric of glass in the window of the basilica in Bonn. Don't you see, Pessoa, the intrusion of quilt-pieces of stained glass. A craftsman tilling with clear glass. Then obscuring part of the view with opaque glass. Leaving both the known and the obscured. The seen and unseen.

At Casa de Luna, I saw the curved shore of the moon. The sky spotted as a coral reef in the sea, though I've never been on the sea. Maybe above it at times. Making motion of immovable structure. Burdened with heavy baggage. Getting it somehow off the ground.

MID-JULY, TEXAS

In the corner of the pasture
in the shade of the tree
the horse waits by his bowl.
It was 105° in the afternoon.
By early evening, it still must be 100°.
The horse has rolled in the dust.
His coat spotted with dirt from the field
where he walks all day eating stubbles of dry grass.
The cicadas drone their noise to summer
scraping legs together as if to get rid of the heat.
The birds flock to their water bowl I set by the house.
In the storage shed I ladle sweet feed
into a bucket I carry to the horse.
He waits in the corner of the pasture grumbling.
He is tired of the flies that surround him.
He is tired of the heat.
I tell him I will pray to the God of temperatures
who is busy overseeing matters of pestilence,
upheaval, war and civil unrest.
He may have neglected
coolant.
He may say he is not responsible.
Whatever I ask
I know his answers remain his own.

Wrangler jeans, chaps, pearl-snap shirt, kerchief, hat,
hat band, square-toed cowboy boots, spurs, socks.

Saddle. Saddle blanket. Stirrup. Cinch. Bridle. Rein.
Lasso. Unpaid bill at Ulysses Bit & Spur. Haybale.
Liniment. Truck. Horse trailer—

"In the first chariot were red horses; and in the second
chariot black horses; and in the third chariot white
horses; and in the fourth chariot grisled and bay horses"—
Zechariah 6:2-3 KJV—

Tangent

BLACK RACER

CATFISH

Box Turtle

Fence Post

FESCUE

Grenadine

Hard Knocks.

TITLED NORTH CENTRAL TEXAS

By the charred warehouse—
  "A Camp in the Prussian Forest"
  RANDALL JARRELL

By the tall field grasses
unmoving at the moment
a gray barn with wide, open door.
A dirt road curves beside the field.
A light-pole leans to the south with a single wire to the outbuilding
as though pulled toward the black hole of the open door.
A blue sky
with a few dangling clouds drift also
toward the low, flat-roofed barn.
I never have walked there to see what is inside.
I stay away from the uncertainty perhaps.
Despite the slow scorn of wind against faith.
The punting against it.
It seems to me
logic
to call upon the unknown one.
To call home.

ACKNOWLEDGMENTS

A Given Grace: An Anthology of Christian Poems, Squircle Line Press, for "The Gospel of Mark Ends Quickly," "Texas Quilt Museum," "Walking on a Cloudy Evening," and "Quiltline"

ANMLY for "Prepare to Die" from the chapter, "The Disruption of Fabric"

Cordite Poetry Review, John Kinsella and Jeanine Leane, editors, Carlton South, Victoria, Australia, for "Tripod"

Craft Literary Creative Nonfiction for Honorable Mention to "Driving Kansas and Texas"

Denver Quarterly Online Folio, FIVES, edited by Billy Stratton, for "Mid-July, Texas," "Two Spirals on the Canyon Wall," "Summons," and "Could We but Lightly Travel"

Gulf Coast for a 2021 finalist to "Two Fields, One to the East of the House, One to the South." Gratefulness to the Chrysostom Society for a first reading, 2022. Acknowledgment also to *When Poets Meet*, Susan Maxwell Campbell and Christine Irving, editors, Denton Poets Assembly, for "Untitled" from which the essay was expanded.

Kansas Speaks Out, Washburn University, Topeka, Kansas, for "Severance," "Hissing in the Leaves," and "In Coldest Weather"

Literature Today for "Body without Language"

LitHub, December 2019 "On Transgression and Writing the Past," interview with Peter Mishler, and *The Midwessy: the Midwest Essay Daily*, March 6, 2021, Ander Monson, for "A Failure to Register Significance," from which various "Fieldnotes" were taken

Martha's Quarterly for "Allusion"

Native Voices at the Autry 2021 Short Play Festival, Los Angeles, for "Where Horses Wear Prom Dresses," from which the second part of "Psalm to Whom(e)" was taken.

Northern Appalachia Review for "Horse"

OEI, Aural Poetics issue, edited by Michael Nardone, for "Cursive— A Trip North" under the title, "Cursive— A Silent Aurality: The Performative Act of Writing." Acknowledgment to Karl Gartung for "Your cursive in water," his video of the edge of Adney Lake in which he caught the sound of handwriting in the waves on his iPhone. Reprinted in "Cursive" by permission.

On the Seawall for "In the Beginning: The Importance of Wildlife in the Development of Human Thought." Gratefulness to Ron Slate for development of the piece.

Pensive Journal for "50 Miles West of Abilene Texas"

Plumwood Mountain, an Australian and International Journal of Ecopoetry and Ecopoetics for "The Horse"

Poetry Society of Texas Annual Anthology for the 2020 first-place award to "Unbound"

Under a Warm Green Linden #14 Indigenous Poetics, edited by Beatrice Szymkowiak for "Untitled North Central Texas" and "Molten Glass Poured on Decomposing Feathers Inside a Round Mold"

Acknowledgment to the Transnational Indigenous Futurities, Literature, Museums, and Digital Territories Conference at Europa-Universität Flensburg, Germany, May 16-18, 2022, for a portion of the chapter, "The Disruption of Fabric."

Gratefulness to Carlow University, Pittsburgh, for a first reading from the manuscript-in-progress, January 2, 2022. Acknowledgment to Carlow also for the field trip to St. Nicolas Croatian Church in "Ablution."

University of Oklahoma Press for permission to reprint "Two Dogs in One" and "The Ball of Fire," from *Cherokee Narratives: A Linguistic Study*, Durbin Feeling, William Pulte and Gregory Pulte, 2018

Ruth Greenstein for the development of the manuscript